AF887050

SONGS of LIFE

SONGS of LIFE

The Poetry of
Susan Evans McCloud

Bookcraft
Salt Lake City, Utah

Copyright © 1985 by Bookcraft, Inc.

All rights reserved. This book or any part thereof may not be reproduced in any form whatsoever, whether by graphic, visual, electronic, filming, microfilming, tape recording or any other means, without the prior written permission of Bookcraft, Inc., except in the case of brief passages embodied in critical reviews and articles.

Library of Congress Catalog Card Number: 85-70702
ISBN 0-88494-563-4

First Printing, 1985

Printed in the United States of America

To my sister

Lora Briggs

whose faith in my poetry

has always been absolute

Of all literary pleasures, the reading of a poem is the highest and purest. Only pure lyric poetry can sometimes achieve the perfection, the ideal form wholly permeated by life and feeling, that is otherwise the secret of music.

—*Hermann Hesse*

Contents

I belong to struggle,
To whirlwind and to fire,
I belong to loneliness,
To longing and desire.

Mist of a Dream

Mist of a dream, on gossamer wings,
Mist of a dream with silver laughter,
I cannot pursue you nor follow after.
I am not worthy to tell your song.
My voice is choked in a narrow throat,
And bounded by mountains and sea and land.
I am not able to take your hand;
My feet are of clay and grounded to earth,
My body is frail and of human birth.

Mist of a dream that comes and goes,
Mist of a dream that grows and hardens,
I cannot shut your music out:
Your song is the voice of the rain and thunder,
The chilling challenge of far-off gods
That wrenches me and tears me asunder
To re-create me, no more mortal,
But leave me trembling, hurt, on fire,
And all strange longing and wild desire.

To Conquer Still

In the gray-blue mist
When the song has died,
And the dream has faded
Beyond the hill,
And the victor's bloody cry is still,
On the far horizon
A light appears,
Pale and faltering—but, oh, so real.
Real to the red-rimmed eyes that seek
And search and hunger,
To eyes that gaze
Beyond the horrors of their own days.
Cease to conquer?
Green hills stretch on.
Beyond the hills there must be dawn.

Declaration

Body . . .
What makes you pompous over me?
What makes you smug,
　　　　so jealous of your power?
I am Wind,
I am Stars,
　　　　bold in a warm night.
I am all the things you cannot be . . .
Like bare gray mountain rock in breathless morning,
A sun-borne seagull,
And screaming creek-foam, awesome in the spring,
Like one soft sigh that hovers on the air
And visits all the hidden, lovely places . . .
I do not need your mock encumbrances,
Your heavy, clumsy flesh.
I am a Voice that sang before I knew you,
I am Music,
　　　　unembodied,
Formless, free.

The Land Around the Corner

The land around the corner is
    a mystery to me,
There's nothing I can learn from it,
    there's nothing I can see
But one broad unbroken vista
    of darkness, deep and still,
I can't make out a garden plot,
    a river or a hill,
I can't send messages ahead,
    nor find a single man
Who's visited, and then returned
    with compass, map, and plan.
No matter what security
    this hour holds for me,
The land around the corner grants
    no gilded guarantee.
It can't be threatened, bribed, nor bought,
    entreated nor enticed,
It holds monopoly on goods
    essential—overpriced.
The land around the corner will
    exact relentless due,
And dangle age-old question marks
    in front of me and you.

This Boat I Row

This boat I row, how do you know
It won't sink down to the sharks below
And spill your life like silver spray—
How do you know another day
Will find you still? You know I steer
A course that's strewn with peril, dear.
You know I sing a gypsy song,
And cannot pay attention long,
And cannot lie as others do.
Oh yes, I will be true to you—
Do sea winds blow? Do night stars rise?
Oh yes, I see your lovely eyes,
Oh yes, I see the anger there,
But I will laugh at your despair,
For I row lightly—don't you know
It doesn't matter where I go,
It doesn't matter what I do,
As long as I am here with you?
It doesn't matter. Row with me,
The best tomorrow's yet to be.
I will not promise safety, dear,
I do not understand your fear.
This boat you row, you row with me
Across a deep, uncharted sea.
It always will be so, I go
Without the vision that you know.
I row, and if I find my way
It will not be because I pray,
It will not be because I do
The thousand things you tie me to.
This boat I row, how do you know
It won't sink down to the sharks below?
How do you know it will not rise
And sail with wings across the skies,
Discovering your dreams for you—
This boat I row on tameless sea?
It well may be, it well may be.

Earth-Star

I tell my story as I tell a dream;
A thing part known, part unknown, part forgot,
A star begun to glimmer, partly seen
And part obscure; as tangible as earth,
And as evasive as a wind-blown wish.
A thought, a sigh, a longing deep desire,
A thing both loved and dreaded, blind and seeing;
An earth-star, both reality and dream.

Strange and wild and sweet and bitter-sweet,
I look into the secrets of my life,
Of what it is and is not and will be,
And might have been—and all are part of me.

In Time

This, too, in time shall pass away,
The pain a memory,
A day we put aside and can't
Recall quite properly.
In time . . . in time—that wicked phrase!
I'd barter twenty years
To drop this burden of despair,
This hour's bitter tears.

Come, Snow

Snow is coming thicker now,
Faster through the sky;
There is not a thing here, snow,
But pain and I.
You can mask the rutted fields,
Muffle bush and tree,
But what kind of succor, snow,
Can you offer me?
You can clog up broadest street,
Blot out friendly lane,
Come, snow, try your powers now
At crushing pain.

Joy is not in things;
it is in us.

—Richard Wagner

Self-Maintenance

And so my spirits rise again,
    With praise and sustenance.
I ought to so maintain myself—
    With my own faith and pride;
I ought to carry sustenance
    Inside.

Isolation

No linnets sang outside my door today,
No gentle rays to chase the gloom away,
No touch of human voice or human hand,
Just the cold wind that screams across the land.

Hide and Seek

I know that I have sinned
against myself,
By walking out on life,
by giving way.
Fog and pain and throbbing,
nagging fear,
Clouds in the skies, and dark clouds
in my mind,
My strengths too tucked away
for me to find.

Discrepancy

Ruin?
    Amid this quiet springtime eve?
Loss?
    When the sun turns gold this lovely room?
Failure?
    Where children's voices lilt and rise?
Despair?
    Where this gentle beauty fills my eyes?

Life As It Is

I have not found Life wanting,
        Just myself.
My own ability to succor joy,
To justify reality with dream,
To see things as they are—
        Not as they seem.

Man's Best Friend

He was not mine, nor was I much to him,
This dog with whom I spent a few stray hours,
Just he and I together at the farm.

Fearful of silence, stiffened with alarm
At unfamiliar sounds, I walked the room,
He a black bulk beside me in the gloom,
Puzzled to walk the empty house with me.

And, once I settled with my poetry,
He thrust his huge gray nose against my hand,
Whining at what he could not understand.

I turned the quiet pages one by one,
Eagerly, for what comfort they might lend,
Uneasily aware that man's best friend,
Watching me now with deep and mournful look,
Offered less comfort than the open book.

What May I Give?

What may I give?
    My dreams blown desolate,
    My heart's desires
    Scattered on the wind,
    And all my faith,
    My vision-strength worn thin.
What may I give?
    That I might breathe,
    Might live?

Thy Ways

I am coming now to know Thee,
Now at last. And trust Thee
Far beyond the hand of flesh.
At last my longings lift,
And I desire Thy blessings
Far above my worldly store.
I want to walk Thy ways with Thee,
And more—I want my spirit
To transcend, to soar.

I am a part of all that I have met.

—Alfred, Lord Tennyson

Touching

I have touched lives today—
New lives
That lift with richness and expectancy,
And old lives I have wallowed in for long,
Old lives that drag me down, deflate my dreams,
Deflect my aim, disintegrate my strength.
The old lives think they know me and hold claim.
Not so.
The new lives feed the inner me
With joy and purpose, touching purity.

The Gift

Everything about me pushes down,
Laughs at me and taunts me with rejection.
Even the skies bring storm and heavy gray.
But then—but then, your letter came today!
How can one spirit lift another so?
What warmth you bring! Will your heart ever know
The sustenance your love and faith impart
To one torn, aching, fearful human heart?

For Me

For me you did not live a year ago,
A month ago . . . Scant days
Have you held place within my heart.
But our two spirits, never quite apart,
Have reached toward this time
When we could blend
In rare affinity and joy again.

Lost River

The River is lost . . .
no one hears her music,
Nor settles, dreaming, in the fragrant grass.
Thick mud has sucked the sap out of her singing,
And quiet hangs a pall on her morass.

The River sleeps . . .
her past is buried, scattered,
I stumble over roots and matted grass,
And sense that something lived here once and flourished,
Thick memories breathe beside me as I pass.

The River wanes . . .
she has no sense of promise,
She spent her golden purpose long ago.
Fearful to disturb the stagnant stillness,
She whispers, and her tones are choked and low.

The River dies . . .
those hearts who lived her loved her,
A fair exchange for sustenance and life.
Sweet dreams were poured into the river's hearing:
Boasts, longings, fears, and madness—none survive.

The River lingers . . .
even love dies slowly,
Something must yet remain to keep her here.
What can she see that lives still to delight her,
Yet shrinks from my veiled sight to disappear?

Untouched

Lonely the woods that knew the
cardinal's song,
Yet heard no sound of human voice
or step,
Lonely the shore where wave washed
after wave,
But never eyes had watched the waves,
and wept.
Lonely the man who, day on day,
alone,
Walked silent—with no song to stir
his own.

Forbidden

The desert doesn't like me.
The rocks, the sand-choked sage—
There seems a soulless anger here
As dry as withered days.
I feel myself forbidden,
This Beauty keeps her pride,
The secrets stirring through the sand
Don't linger to confide.
The desert doesn't like me—
I haven't come to stay—
My footsteps on the trackless waste
Blow soundlessly away.

Keep thy heart with all diligence;
For out of it are the issues of life.

—*Proverbs 4:23*

Proficiency

Not yet,
But I am moving,
Lifting.
The blue air
Is fresh and pure.
Not yet,
But I am learning
To rejoice
As I endure.

Today

I am strong again—
Today I gave,
And forced my own
Anxieties aside,
And bared my heart
To beauty
And to love,
And listened
To the sounds
Of my own soul;
Today I gave—
And found
My own heart whole.

Reminder

Danger and discouragement,
    Failure and despair,
Trials to keep us humble,
    To help us stay aware
That triumph starts with struggle,
    And strength can grow from pain,
And oh, how bright the sun that breaks
    Through shadow, mist, and rain!

Face to Face

Do crazy things—
    Go on,
Take chances,
    Dare!
Let dreams drown out
    Blind caution's
Soothing tone.
    Be!
Though you tremble,
    Exposed . . .
Storm-tossed . . .
    Alone . . .

Old Leaves

The tree outside this doorway
Against this spot of sky
Has just a few leaves clinging,
Brown leaves up high.

I have a few leaves clinging,
Bleached, brittle, in my mind,
Old leaves that winter's bitter wind
Can't ferret out and find.

They serve me no good purpose,
And yet, if one should fall,
I'd feel a loss, a loneliness
I can't explain at all.

All That Was

Today the sun shone pale upon the snow,
The air was cold, the sky hung misty-gray,
And nothing seemed to mark the time, no show
That something old was dying with the day.

Today shall whisper off into the grave.
The little human store of hope and fear
Shall sigh and linger, crowding anxious hearts
That would discard it with the played-out year.

Men raise their toasts, and laugh into the dawn,
And call the day a new and wondrous thing,
But all that was continues and goes on,
Hearts lull again . . . and lips forget to sing.

Return to School

Bunker Hill was not retained,
Nor the asphalt sea
Where nameless little boys and girls
Played so carelessly.
But I walked through the silent halls
And up the sweeping stair,
Listening for voices
That were no longer there:
Shadow children in the rooms,
Shadow memory,
A little girl with wide brown eyes
Stood staring back at me.
She hadn't written any books,
She hadn't found her way,
She didn't know how many trials
Would come before this day.
But we looked out the windows
At the spired view together,
Dreaming, as she used to,
Lost in fairyland.
Then she turned her soft brown eyes on me—
And took my hand.

Love is a passion which kindles
honor into noble acts.

—John Dryden

The Bird of Longing

The bird of longing came to me
On wings of silver touched with mist,
I sighed to leave my infant dreams,
Yet I could not resist.

The bird of longing came to me,
I could not bid him stay his flight,
I had to leave my budding dreams
And follow, whether wrong or right.

Some wander in the fields of love,
And walk the gardens of desire,
And sing strange songs into the night
To tempt the bird of fire.

I only kissed the morning dew,
With eager plans of things to be,
And walked in light, and never knew
The bird of love would come to me.

This Love

So many verses come to me with ease,
But what I feel for you is hard to say,
Is so bound up with what I am inside:
Ten years ago and more, I was your bride,
Lovely and young and certain of my love.
How could the years have brought such varied times,
Such patterns that have formed us on our way?
My love for you is not the same today
As when we started—that love was untried,
And new, with only faith to chart its course.
This love I hold has known much fear and pain,
Much tenderness and joy, all woven through
The fibre of my being. Ah, more true
And bright and long-abiding is this love,
That moves between us like soft melody,
Murmuring hushed promises of eternity.

The Plea

These, our dark days, have lived because of you.
How many times I've drunk your love and praise
As one who thirsts and cannot ever fill!
But in my highest moments when I thrill
To the best love and knowledge I possess,
I love you with such purity and joy!
Yet sometimes fears and weaknesses destroy
The sustenance and love I wish to give.
We have a long eternity to grow,
But there's so much I want to give you now!
Remember as I struggle—know, somehow,
My love for you is deep and warm and true.
It sings and lifts and grows—and learns from you.

Young Mother

I wanted this;
    I walked so strong,
So blithely
    Through the soft, fair
Morning hours.
    Failure an unconsidered
Possibility,
    Fear . . . Uncertainty?
It's morning still,
    But day is quickly
Pushing out the dawn;
    All my bright young
Certainty
    Is gone.
Love weaving chains?
    So light, so sure,
Chains fastened to
    A woman's naked heart.
If I lost you
    To death,
To sin, to pain . . .
    Night's darkness would
Engulf me.
    Stay the hours,
I pray now,
    And I tread more carefully.
I need this daylight time
    To walk with you,
To stroke your golden heads,
    To fill you, love you
Now, while you are here!
    The darkness creeps . . .
The darkness is so near.

You Four

You Four . . .
I stride as whirlwind through your days,
Angry, self-seeking, willing hurt and pain—
And then, again, I move in gentle peace,
Soft to sustain, lovely to laugh and lift,
Bearing the strength of patience in my hand.

You Four . . .
Can your hearts ever understand
The woman who walks restlessly between
The earth-bound mortal and the visioned dream?

Awareness

Mother, my love for you is more than
last year's love,
Deeper, more tender,
For I have seen my heart
Laid bare to pain and fear
I never knew—
Uncertainties. And then
I thought of you—
Who did endure,
Who somehow still possess
A vernal faith,
A singing gentleness.
I see new things,
harmonious and fair,
More of you, Mother—
the You
That was always there.

My Kingdom

You may close the door upon me,
And think when you are gone,
"Poor thing, she's stuck at home all day,"
How wrong, my dear, how wrong!

I am queen of my own castle,
I hold expectant sway,
For I decree what things will fill
The hours of my day.

There are diapers, true, and dishes,
And work that must be done,
But Mozart keeps me company
And makes it seem like fun.

I can take a walk with baby
Whenever I may please,
And watch the robins peck for worms,
And taste the sweet spring breeze.

Or I may sit by the window,
My Byron on my knee,
And wander strange enchanted dreams
Of worlds that used to be.

I've clothes to mend and tears to dry,
Toys strewn across my floor,
But I have children's laughter, too,
And who could ask for more?

You come home to me, dear, tired
From a world that is cold,
But I have angel lips to kiss,
And golden heads to hold,

And little arms about my neck,
And whispers in my ear.
Your world outside my castle walls
Can't hold such treasures, dear.

Mary

Even I am a woman, as all other women,
And tonight I feel awkward and cold and afraid.
The hurt binds my breath, my body is heaving,
And the anguish wrings tears of pain.
But oh, this ecstasy . . . how this ecstasy?
This weakness I feel when I touch his face?
The softness, the wonder that he lies here breathing,
Warm and pulsing within my embrace?

So this is the beauty that lights my countenance,
This the knowledge that burns in my eyes,
This the joy that pulses my being,
Transforming my body and heart and brain.
There are people here, and noise and speaking—
But he and I lie apart and alone.
Joseph smiles and speaks to me silently;
I think he knows, I think he knows.

I perceive that this baby is different, special,
I know he belongs to his people, and God,
But he is my firstborn; exquisite, divine.
Tonight there is no one—prophets nor angels—
For I am his mother . . . and he is mine.

Beauty is the highest expression
of morality.

—Frank Lloyd Wright

Morning Song

Sometimes when daylight sifts to gray,
And all the world lies silent,
We listen to the stillness sounds
That seem to seep from underground
And weave a warmth around us.

Sometimes when winter crackles cold,
We snuggle near the fire,
And mother reads of olden days,
Her voice like silk; a golden haze
Transports me back to other days.

And I know feelings soft and new
That taste like dreams and promises come true.

One Rose

One rose is all you need, one new green tree
Whose branches trace a pattern on the sky,
One lilac bush to scent the passing breeze—
I have been long content with such as these.

One spray of bridal wreath across the lawn,
One berry to stain juice upon your hand,
One meadow lark to sing what he may please—
I find myself content with such as these.

Beauty is beauty, let her come to me
Enough to feed the dream and tune the heart,
Enough that I drop down upon my knees—
Happy to be content with such as these.

The Half-Moon

The half-moon wasn't yellow,
The half-moon wasn't gold,
It smouldered like a ducat
From the pirate ships of old.

It smouldered burnished copper,
It smouldered scarlet red,
It sent its piercing arrow lights
Like music through my head.

The moon was a bright gypsy
That danced through tattered cloud,
The wind wove silver through the sky
And laughed out loud.

I felt the wild sky tremble,
I heard the dark earth sigh,
And there was nothing breathing
But eternity and I.

Protest

They say the world is dying,
But I can feel a strain,
A thrill of pure, ecstatic life
That no one can explain.

There's something in the color,
There's something in the taste
Of autumn's breath on cheek and hair
That winter cannot waste.

If autumn is a dying,
Then dying must be joy,
A wild brave show of splendor
That nothing can destroy.

I live, I thrive on autumn
Intensely. Death may call,
But beauty such as I feel here
Can never die at all.

The Edges of My Soul

The crows and I keep vigil here
Against the winter sky,
And there is something in my throat
And something in their cry
That speaks of spirits soaring
Beyond the bounds of pain,
Yet bearing man's old loneliness
To pull them down again,
Never certain if the tears,
The quickening of heart,
Come of joy or hunger
Too sweeping to control.
And so the crows fly crying
Round the edges of my soul.

When she had passed it seemed like
the ceasing of exquisite music.

—Henry Wadsworth Longfellow

Together

We walked together, Sarah, worlds ago,
And dreamed and planned and dared so much together,
And in your purity you trusted me
To guide you through the mists you could not see.
You trusted me, and chose to bless my life.
If I could just remember how it felt
To smooth your hand and kiss your lips—and go,
So eager to prepare the way for you!
The pain was something we could not imagine,
The pain I need to purify me, too.
But oh, the joy that thrilled us long ago—
You brought that joy and left it here with me.
Your little body, beautiful and frail,
Shall someday clothe your spirit's majesty,
It is a loving, humble gift from me—
Your body, and my pain and love and joy.
I smooth your tiny hand, then let it go.
I kiss your lips . . . So briefly did you stay,
And hold my hand, and walk this mortal way.
But spirits do not part so easily . . .
Your hand is warm in mine, and now I know
Your spirit always has been close to me,
Firm are the bonds that bind us soul to soul,
Old bonds—and new.
We walk together, Sarah, mother and child,
Sisters. We walk together in the light,
And I shall never face the dark alone,
For I shall always feel your presence near,
Your warmth shall as a shield encircle me,
Your pulse, your light—just there—
Promise of all the tomorrows we will share.

The Vigil

The two small pine trees stand apart,
Like graceful, growing sentinels,
And they tend well the little rise
Where Sarah's lovely body lies.
Already we are friends—they speak
In subtle moans and sighs and creaks.
Whispering, my wounded heart replies.

The years will pass and they shall grow
Sturdy and tall while I grow frail,
And they shall keep their vigil well,
As I keep mine: Through warmth and green,
Through winter's ice and weight of snow,
Through rain and thunder, tempest-blown,
The little form is not alone.
Nor is the spirit—she walks free,
In love and harmony with me.

Illumination

A year ago I spent this day in pain,
And anxious expectation of release;
So gently and so easily you came,
Bringing a sense of wonder and of peace.

You came—but not to stay and fill my days,
Your little body failed our eager plan,
Your life had different purposes and ways,
Our brief time fled before it scarce began.

Today would mark your first year on this earth,
But time has left me only memory,
Time that could mould the hour of your birth
Then speed you into death, ahead of me.

A year ago I did not dream today
Could happen, could have place in the design;
But then I did not know this kind of love,
With power to sustain, uplift, refine.

One More

Four little girls, and their eyes are bright,
Their voices laugh and sing,
Four little girls walk by my side,
Such happiness they bring.

Everyone greets us when we pass,
As kindly as can be.
Four little girls with their mother,
And that is all they see.

People smile on the four little girls,
But no one seems to know
One more small girl walks by my side
Wherever I may go.

The Promise

Today it doesn't seem like spring—
It's raining flakes of snow;
Five years ago spring came with you,
With new delights to show.

I didn't think of parting then,
But just of how you came,
Of how our lives and spirits now
Would never be the same.

Five springs, five lazy summers since,
Five winters on the land—
But that spring day five years ago
I held your tiny hand,

And I promised you forever,
With lovely springs to spare.
The promise will not fade, my dear,
Forever still is there.

As You

March wears away his bluster,
And the spring
Bursts every boundary to spill her joy
In beauty much too beautiful to hold,
As you . . .
Whose lovely tale was briefly told.

Every heart sings the sweet
Elusive song,
While spring, too frail, too fair to linger long,
Will glide away upon a gentle breeze,
As you . . .
Who left me softly like the spring.

Her Last Spring

Her last spring wasn't spring at all.
April was December.
And never had there been such rain
Since people could remember.

May drowned in rain and valley snows,
And bitter was the cold.
The blossoms on the lilac bush
Would never quite unfold.

And yet what better did she have?
She sat upon his knee
And smelled the grass and shivered some—
There wasn't much to see.

No flags, no early roses yet.
He took her back inside.
And without aid of peach or phlox
She closed her eyes and died.

Stamp of Her

Everything here has stamp of her upon it:
The comfy cluttering, the casual air,
The useful things left standing here and there
For when she may have need of them. She loved
Whatever came to her; she was not fussy,
Not one to have her way—she took each hour,
Each passing day, and gave the best she could.

It doesn't seem that here she could be gone.
As long as there are birds that come to feed,
And fill the pleasant country with their song—
As long as children swarm where once she fed,
Though gone—not seen—not heard—
She is not dead.

We are born for a higher destiny
than that of earth.

—*Edward G. Bulwer-Lytton*

Answered Prayer

Little one, I prayed for you before the time you came.
Aren't a waiting mother's prayers always the same?
Let this child be healthy, please let him be all right!
A woman's anguished pleadings into the silent night.

Then you came; not healthy, but more perfect than I knew,
I wondered what the Lord had done, sending me you.
What about my foolish prayers, had they all been in vain?
He had listened, knowing He was sending me pain.

It took a while to understand, a while to see
What a blessing heaven had held in store for me.
I had wanted something less, not knowing you were there,
Nor all the tender love that stood behind my answered
prayer.

Going Home

Mourn not for me, for I am going home.
No more will lonely fears disturb my sleep,
No longer will thick darkness clog my steps,
Nor tears my eyes. You sigh because you know
That I shall never see another spring.
Is beauty something of the earth alone,
Confined to bone and flesh? These eyes have known
A beauty that still sings within my dreams,
A promise of things lost. My spirit aches,
Restless now for release. You look and see
The wasted, withered shell through which you knew
The breath of the Eternal that is me . . .
But deep within, where mortal eyes can't see,
The young and vital spirit still holds sway,
And age does not exist—I'm going home
To all the things I've missed. Mourn not for me,
For you still bow beneath the yoke of fear
And pain, but me—I'm going home again!

Vermont 1805

Upon that day a mighty spirit moved the heavens
And all the great and high ones gathered there.
One noble spirit now approached the Father—
Alone, in all his grandeur—
Unafraid.
He eagerly received the Father's blessing.
Respectfully the others moved aside
With prayers, exultant lauding
As he passed from out their midst
And took his way below.

And on that day a lowly man in Vermont
Received a son.
The weary mother smiled in deep content.
The day was cold with snow and brumal winds.
They laid him in a cradle of hewn wood
And called him Joseph—after his great fathers.

This Joseph

It happened in another time, I know,
And in a place where I have never been.
I did not see the man nor hear his voice,
But what I am, I am because this Joseph,
In spite of youth, in spite of fear and trials,
Became a prophet of the living God.

The living God—I know my Father lives,
I know I am his child, I know my place
Because the prophet saw him face to face,
Because he had the faith to seek the truth,
And loved both man and God enough to die
That truth might live, prevail and magnify.

I love this man; his spirit speaks to me
Past all the many years that part our lives.
I know that Joseph was a man of God,
I know because my spirit soars with joy.
I test his words and find the truth can stand,
I pray and feel the Spirit warm my soul,
For I have made these truths my very own
To light me as I walk the pathway home.

The Mormon Mother

I. Nauvoo

She stood upon the ice-imprisoned bank,
And clasping stiff, numbed hands she
let her eye
Strain past the frigid river and seek out
The stately form of russet brick—
her home,
Its windows shining in the dimming rays;
Remembered all held dear within those walls;
Took one deep breath, then forced
her eyes away,
To seek with pride the lofty temple spire,
Celestial-white against the darkened sky,
Erect in bold defiance of the world.
Embracing all the sight within her mind,
Kept vivid there, she turned, with
lifted head,
To start her journey down the waiting trail.

II. The Trek

Beside the frozen grave, so roughly dug,
She stood, and let the tears come to
her eyes,
And did not stop them when they wet
her cheeks,
A moment only. She could bear no more.
Forever passed until she turned away.
And then, with nimble, knowing hands
she worked,
With toughened, mud-caked feet walked
resolute,
With stiffened lips she spoke, with
trained ears heard,
And saw within her heart the lonely grave,
Another hurt; yet she denied it not,
But kept it as companion to the pain.

III. The Valley

On humble knee she lifted thankful eyes,
Then rested them on emptiness and space,
On rugged crags and burning mountain sage—
The barren valley far below. But faith
Within her own breast surged with
strength anew,
Transformed the desert to a blossoming
rose:
To homes, to fruitful fields, schools,
streams, and roads,
A temple—all rose up before her eyes.
Within her heart this precious vision
grew
And overshadowed those already there,
Granting a brightness to their
pain-dulled hues,
And lent her winged feet as she descended
The last long mountain, to the
valley home.

This Is My Day

My day began in scant-remembered yesterdays ago,
My day moves on and outward
like a river in its flow,
My day embraces more than where I am,
and what I do,
And all those that I love, and have loved,
form a part of my day too.

This is my day, and much of it I do not know or see.
All I have done or will do
are a part of what is me.
And there is love which waits for me in forms
I do not know,
Those I shall love are part of how my day
will live and grow.

This is my day—and it shall move and lift
and sing along,
And all the loves and learnings of my life
shall shape its song:
This is my day.